# DARK GLASSES

(Another book financed on my
hopes and paid for with my tears)

# DARK GLASSES

Dan Hendrickson

A Sticky Hat Production
in association with
Lemon Town LTD.

Produced by Flat Sole Studio
398 Goodrich Avenue, St. Paul, MN 55102
*www.flatsolestudio.com*

Copyright © 2017 Dan Hendrickson

All rights reserved. No part of this publication
may be reproduced in whole or in part
without written permission of the publisher.

**Photo Credits**
Mackenzie Kelley, pg. 16
Deb Sjurseth, pg. 130
Amy Hendrickson, back cover photo
All other photos by Henry Rifle

**Art Direction**
Amy Hendrickson
Henry J. Rifle
Deb Sjurseth

**Book and Cover Design**
Flat Sole Studio

**Video Production Team**
Chanzie, LLC

Lyrics to Bleed True reprinted courtesy of Sagebrush Records

NOTE: The Rosanne Cash lyric is correct—I checked.

For booking information, contact Dan at Dan1812@hotmail.com.

To Amy, Will and Soren, as well as my family and friends

To Darci, Mark and Todd, who read this when it was just a bucket of cold gray malarkey (as opposed to the Monochromatic Marvel it is now)

To my co-workers, past and present, all of whom I adore (Be-Be-Be!)

To Kris and Jim, the Optometrists who loaned me the eye blocker . . . thingie

To my golf cronies (you know who you are)

To Vanislaw, Schmidty, Dusty, Chad and Nate

To the Moes (fuhgeddaboutit)

To Noah G., Kurtsauce and Tonysmithburger™

To Oliver Hart and everyone else doing time on the Weird Side

To Dick Tuck

To Francis Xavier Flynn, Arkady Renko and Herbert Nenninger

To Blake Hoena and the gang at Flat Sole Studio

And, of course, to Spec Four, Dean Keaton and Hal 9000 in the Year 2000 and 10

"... and we'll fill in the missing colors/in each other's paint-by-number dreams. And then we'll put our dark glasses on ..."
—Jackson Browne, *The Pretender*

"Well, I've got the guts to fool them/given half the chance."
—Bash and Pop, *Never Aim to Please*

I once crushed a pair of my glasses (prescription) because I was convinced I was looking at the world wrong. That should give you some idea of where I've been. Where I'm going, that's tougher to ~~say~~ see.

# An Introduction

### My Name is
My name is Dan Hendrickson,
and I'm a poet, a sponge
and a canteen.
People tell me I can't
be all three.
I say, "*Watch me.*"


### Not Much to Tell
I like to have a drink or three,
I'm pretty good with words and
I have
no shame whatsoever.
And so
I became
a poet.


### The Thinker
When I stop to think about it,
I've always been a little bit
confused.
I was born scratching my head.
Mom still hasn't
forgiven me.

*Time spent off the radar is the best time to learn how to fly.*

Dan Hendrickson

**Trial Balloons**
Sometimes I pretend
to start talking.
Just to see if anyone
is listening.


**Early Warning System**
My poetry is a lot like
the rain that shows up
on radar
but evaporates long before
it ever hits the ground.
In other words, you won't need
an umbrella,
but you might
need a canteen.
And when the clouds roll past
and the words fade away,
it will be tough to tell
what, if anything,
happened.


**Bureau of Land Management**
It would probably
be a lot easier
to have a clear-cut mind.
But I prefer to keep mine
dense and overgrown.
The ideas that do
make it out
are robust, hearty.
They've been through it.
They know
what it's about.

### Eff Scott Fitzgerald
Halfway through writing this book,
I had a fairly major breakdown.
I hit the wall—real hard.
After a scattershot recovery,
I met up with a good friend I hadn't seen
in a while and filled him in on
what all had happened, to the point
that I could explain it.
He was very cool about it,
responding simply by saying,
"*Well, at least now you finally have
something in common with
F. Scott Fitzgerald.*"
Friends are great that way,
always slicing right
through the clutter
and cutting
straight to the bone.


### My Back Pages
You perhaps see a complete fossil
dinosaur skeleton
assembled neatly
on the spotless, gray
museum floor.
I see another pile of bones
that, more likely than not,
just wanted
to be left alone.

Dan Hendrickson

**Fossil Record**
There's only a handful
of glamour
in this bare-knuckle world
and I've never cared
enough to fight
for much of it.
I figure, in time,
your bony fingers
will extend
just as fruitlessly
as mine.


**The Crack-up**
My most recent breakdown
was a long time coming.
Just for example, my Spanish nickname
has long been San Andreas.
And there were no shortage
of other complicating factors.
Many to do with issues of identity.
To start with, everyone called me Danny
growing up.
Then in junior high, one of the first girls
that ever showed interest in me
suggested that I shorten my name
to Dan,
which I did, without question.
What can I tell you?
She smacked my butt
from time to time.
It would have been impolite not
to change my given name.

# Dark Glasses

### Party of One
My name *is* Dan Hendrickson,
and I'm a poet and a philosopher.
Although my poet friends tell me
I'm really more of a philosopher
and my philosopher friends
say I'm actually more of a poet.
At the end of any given day,
I'm never really sure whether
anyone truly likes me or not.
But, I keep forging blindly ahead.
That's the American Way!


### Pleased to Meet Me
I used to like to wear
sunglasses
and pretend, if only for a little while,
that I was someone else.
Someone more . . .
I don't even know, what?
But then we all like
to do that
sometimes.
Do we not?


### Say Anything
Some people think
I just might
have something to say.
I don't know
about that.
A person hears
so many things.
It's tough
to know what
to believe.

Dan Hendrickson

**Professional Courtesy**
I've seen dead people
every single day of my life
as I've humped my way through time.
But I've never really said
too much about it.
Frankly, I always thought it was
none of my business
and, therefore, just kept moving
right along.
But lately, more and more,
it's occurred to me that
maybe
I've had that
all wrong.



**Vessels**
Sometimes
we're the bottle,
sometimes
we're the ship,
occasionally,
we're the cork
but always
we're adrift.




*Most folks are like clipper ships, trapped in bottles—*
*stuck fast. I'm here to break some glass.*

# Dark Glasses

**Occluder**
Anybody can memorize
an eye chart.
It doesn't mean
you have vision.

*The great thing about giving yourself vision tests—you always pass.*

# THE SHUFFLE

### Sung In the Key of Benjamin Franklin
I'm an artist,
people should love me.
So why don't they?
That's what me and my therapist
spent a lot of time trying
to figure out recently.
At least one of us was trying.
I'm pretty sure about that.
Yes, I really dug deep.
I 'did the work.'
All in the hopes of
calling down
that lightning bolt revelation
to make it all
make sense.


### J. J. Pickle
If you give people a choice
between a poet and a pickle,
most people
will choose the pickle.
Pickles are generally
far tastier, less crunchy.
and much easier
to digest.

Dan Hendrickson

**Blasé**
At one of my first counseling sessions,
my therapist said to me,
*"Even if you had something to say*
*. . . who would listen?"*
I had to admit he had me stumped
as far as that.
Then he returned his focus
to the crossword puzzle he was working on,
although not before asking me
if I knew
a five-letter word for indifferent.
I'm still working on that one.
I'm still working on a whole bunch of stuff,
actually.


**Thank You, Edvard Munch**
I'm a long ways past
wanting to know
what any of it
means.
In fact,
if someone who knew
came along
and tried
to tell me now,
I promise you,
I would scream.

## Natural Fluctuations

Every time I think I've
gained weight,
people tell me that
it looks like
I've lost weight.
And every time I think
I've lost weight,
someone walks up to me,
places two hands on my
belly, proceeds to shake it
like a Magic 8-Ball
and says, "*Uh-oh! Looks like
someone's put on a little love!*"
I don't get this place.
And it's becoming clearer
by the day
I never will.


## ST/100/6

Trying to get
your head around
this place is tough.
It's like trying to get
a head-sized pillowcase
around a world-sized
pillow.
You see what I'm saying.
Sure, it might be possible, but
it would require
the absolute right kind of fabric.
And as sweet as it might feel,
cheap Velour isn't going to cut it.

Dan Hendrickson

**Down Goes Frasier**
I always like to tell folks,
'I don't mind
going to dark places
—especially if it's for a good cause!'
and that statement is true.
See, I've been dark places.
Places where the sun
was little more
than a dim afterthought.
Like the time, just for instance,
when I could physically feel
my mind
begin to unwind at its very base,
like fresh cotton candy being
peeled away from its cardboard cone.
It began with something someone said,
a sentence which echoed very strangely
in the back of my head,
and seemed to lead only down,
someplace very bad.
Thankfully, the process stopped
long before it could finish.
It was somewhat like being in a funhouse
without mirrors. And where's the fun in that?
They should call it a sadhouse.
If you ask me.


**Kreskin**
No one's ever tried
to read my mind,
which is fortunate.
I can't even read my mind.
It's like Sanskrit!
Fact of it is,
I never know what I'm thinking
—until it's too late.

Dark Glasses

### In the Midst
In the midst of my most recent
personal difficulties,
I remember looking at myself
in the mirror and thinking,
"*Well, well, well. How about this?
The Prince of Laughs can't find
a smile.*"
Oh. Yeah.
That's probably something else
I should tell you.
I sometimes call myself
The Prince of Laughs.


### To Be Very Clear
By 'Prince of Laughs,'
I don't mean THE Prince.
I mean the normal kind.
The kind you would
cheerfully pants
if the Queen wasn't watching.


### Avalon
I wear my blandness
like a suit of armor.
King Arthur himself
never had it so good!


### Valley Forge
Swords naturally
dislike
the forging process.
But cannot argue
their subsequent sharpness.

Dan Hendrickson

**Satellite Clown**
Some time ago,
I was flipped,
not unlike a standard playing card,
far out beyond the limits
of our thin atmosphere,
into cold, dark space.
Like a casually discarded
Jack of Hearts,
I suppose you could say.
All I can say now is
thank goodness
for sweet gravity.
On the other hand, about
all that's left of me
is the stuff that didn't burn up
on re-entry.


**Remainder**
I've found myself on the
outside
of more equations
than even the most devoted
statistician
would care to count.
Now, it's true that I'm no
William L. Burke,
but trust me,
I know exactly
how numbers work.

### A Simple Mathematical Principle
You can't be a good person
and a good poet.
It's not possible.
Something's
got to give.

### My Name is Jonah
Sometimes you have to be
swallowed by a whale
in order to subsequently
be spit out by that same whale.
I know that doesn't make much
sense, but it's a complicated system.
I don't make the rules.

### Beach Party
Whenever I'm at the ocean
and see kids playing with
a beach ball,
the first thing I think is,
*"A whale's probably going
to choke to death on that."*
I'm a lot of fun at parties.
People love me.

Dan Hendrickson

**My Name is Wepeel!**
Sometimes when you
follow your heart
you wind up inside
the belly of
a great whale.
But, to be fair,
the very same thing can
happen
when you buy
a Road Atlas.
Weary travelers receive
no guarantees.
At least none
that I'm aware of.


**Belushi Whale**
I hate when you're enjoying
a perfectly nice walk
along the beach,
and everything's sunny and just
the best,
when you step into a stinky
heap of ambergris.
Friggin' sperm whales.
I think you know what I'm saying.


**Encryption Key**
I've noticed, over the years,
that people I don't know
will often smile at me
when we pass on the street.
And I can never figure that out.
Until I remember that they
don't have access
to the same files I do.

Dark Glasses

**Harpoon Blues**
Some people
like to poke things
with sticks.
They think it's fun.
That's not at all my thing.
I've been poked
with sticks before.
There's nothing fun
about it.


**Mire Lane**
Some people
sink a long ways
down into themselves,
and not everyone
knows how to swim
or even tread water;
all the little tricks it takes
to survive, endure.
That is one way
to learn, though.
That's for damn sure.

Dan Hendrickson

**Creature From**
In my younger days,
I used to wonder why women
didn't want me.
Now I think I get it.
I was the walking equivalent
of an emotional drift net.
A lovelorn La Brea Tar Pit!
Anyone who so much as tiptoed in
even lightly
would have sunk straight down
to the bottom of all that muck
and goo.
I only barely managed to
escape myself.
And let me just add,
I think what they say
about cigarettes
is true.
All that tar . . .
it's no good for your lungs.


**DNA**
A lot of people
think they know me.
As far as those people go,
I have only two questions:
Where did you meet me?
What was I
wearing
at the time?


*I'm a poor man's Butch Cassidy. Henry Rifle was my Sundance Kid.*

Dark Glasses

### A Little Paint Goes a Long Way
Clowns do good work.
They make us question
not only the choices we've made,
but also the choices they've made.
Yes, clowns do important work.
They make us think, whether
we care to or not.


### Swirl
When a clown
meets a shark
there's always a
colorful exchange
of ideas.


### Smoke and Mirrors
You can give a clown
a cigarette,
but you know
they're just going to
do something
annoying as hell with it.
So I say you might as well
smoke the goddamn thing
yourself.
The FDA might well disagree
with me on this,
but I think it's
a healthier choice.


*A rake will never savor the heights, but it will know the taste of leaves.*

# THE DEAL

# Dark Glasses

> *"Who were you then, who are you now?"*
> —The Pretenders, *Talk of the Town*

### All You Can Eat
I was . . . I'm sure, as excited as anyone
else on graduation night.
High school has to lead
somewhere, right?
That's the notion, at least.
I was finishing up a chat
with a good friend of mine
when
an adult I didn't know
sidled up beside me and said,
*"Young man, enjoy this night.
Life is a feast where
victory is the appetizer
and the main course is defeat."*
He clapped me on the back, then,
and whispered, soft and light,
*"I hope you brought your appetite."*


### Chameleon Tea
I'm a relatively
easy-going fellow.
But I don't tell
many people that.
I'm afraid
they might steal
my wallet.

*If your vision is clear enough, everyone can see.*

Dan Hendrickson

**Fiber Optics**
If I have one strength
as a writer, it's this:
I trust my eyes.
I know what I see
when I see it.


**Rabbit's Foot**
Years ago . . .
God, forever ago,
I was driving out
past the Fargo (ND) airport
towards the end of another brutal winter.
It was still freezing out and
lying in the very middle of
the road
was the body
of a thoroughly deceased
rabbit.
He or she died in such a way
that a mangled front paw
was left sticking up, rather grotesquely,
as though it were saying,
to all those driving over its corpse,
*"Hey, there! How's it goin'?"*
And I remember thinking,
*"Better than you, my furry friend
—just a little."*


**Keeping Them in Suspense**
My grandfather was a magician,
but he wasn't very good.
It took him 80 years
to disappear.

### Clown Shoes
I visited my bank recently.
When one of the tellers noticed me,
she gave me a look.
"*What do YOU want?*" she snapped.
"*Oh, just . . . looking for free stuff,*" I replied,
nonchalantly.
She frowned then, returning her attention
to the stack of large bills she was counting out.
Yes, if there's one thing people
truly value and respect on this planet,
it's creativity.


### Life of the Party
Having an offbeat comic perspective
is sometimes useful, I'll admit.
It can come in handy at parties
and wakes.
But what it doesn't do is pay the rent.
You can ask my landlord about that.
If you see him, tell him I've almost
got last month's rent scraped together.
But be careful when you do.
Look him in the eye, nice and level.
He can smell a lie two miles away.
I swear,
the man's the devil!


### Welcome Wagon
I'm fairly informal
in bed.
I call people
by their first names.

*Everybody loves a clown but no one pays his bills.*

Dan Hendrickson

**Upon Further Reflection**
There was this guy who always
used to outsmart me.
One day I said, "*Do you think
you're smart because you can
outsmart me?*"
"*Oh, no!*" he said. "*Absolutely not.*"
It wasn't until later that I realized
he had outsmarted me again.


**Buck Henry**
I sleep naked because . . .
frankly, I think a lot of people
have come to expect it from me.
Do I think that it makes
me a better person?
I don't know.
You tell me, Dr. Phil*.
You seem to have all the answers.


**Rules and Then Rules**
Bank girls are pretty
and have all the money,
but they
can't touch
much of it.

*Dr. Phil was a bald guy who, at least for a short time,
some people actually seemed to listen to.

Dark Glasses

**In the Game**
Let me tell you,
things have changed a lot
since I was "in the game."
Back in my day,
we didn't have
email, e-Harmony
or drunk-texting
to find companionship.
No siree.
We had to pick
our dates up
in public places, like
The Post Office,
city parks
and bus stations.
Before we
took them home
and banged them.

Dan Hendrickson

**Time Passages**
I'm old enough to remember
when you got a room key
when you checked into a hotel.
An actual key,
not just some generic access card.
Those were the days.
We thought the universe was ours.
How little we knew.
How little
we knew.


**True Romance (AKA Bash and Pop)**
A lot of people treat sex
like it's some sort of demolition derby.
No touch, no creativity, no finesse.
It's just bump, bump, bump;
smash, smash, smash.
I've never understood
that philosophy,
not even once.
I mean,
we have the room
for an hour.
What's the rush?

## Toe in the Water

For a long time,
sex kind of scared me.
I'm not sure I'd say I found it
distasteful or anything like that,
but some squeamishness definitely
factored into it.
Unbridled passion,
bodily fluids,
things that are rigid . . .
It's no place for a gentleman.


## Nobleman

I always like it when
a woman who thinks
she knows me—but doesn't—
comes up behind me at the mall
and gives me a playful slap on the ass.
It only happened once, I guess,
and she was SO embarrassed
I just smiled and said,
*"Hey, no need to apologize.*
*Daddy likes it hot!"*
It's funny.
Someone I don't know
comes up behind me and slaps
MY ass, and I'm the one who
gets asked to leave Barnes and Noble.
What am I missing here?
What's wrong with this picture?!

Dan Hendrickson

**Leaders Lead**
Life is like that time
when you shouted,
*"Let's all go skinny dipping!"*
And then proceeded to strip
off your clothes and charged,
completely naked, out into the water
and no one followed you.
They all just stood on the beach
and stared while you tried to keep
all your best parts submerged.
After a while . . . yeah,
it just gets awkward.


**Just Like Everyone Else**
I have no problem
getting naked for
massages, but
I tend to avoid
nude beaches.
I'll say it to you like this:
If you want to see
my junk . . .
you're going
to have to pay for it.

# Dark Glasses

**Van Helsing**
There are only two cardinal rules
for male poets.
1) Never let them
see you sweat
and
2) Never let them
see your balls.
And no matter how hard I try,
I always seem to break at least
one of those rules.

Sometimes two.


**Practicality**
I don't believe
in bucket lists.
Or buckets, for that matter.
Buy a hose,
for chrissake.


**Man Cave**
This might surprise some people,
but I have a "Man Cave."
As these things go, it's
fairly androgynous.
The only things in there
are an old falafel maker,
a diving board
and an industrial laminating machine.
I don't spend
a whole lot of time down there.
The place really gives me the creeps.

Dan Hendrickson

**The Naked Truth**
Being a poet isn't all that
different
from being a stripper.
You get up onstage and
you do your thing, and
people either respond
to what you're doing
or they don't.
Either way, at the end of the night,
you put your clothes back on and
—after you've
shifted your car into drive—
you go home.
And at least
you can say
that you tried.


**Daily Rind**
"*And your obsession with lemons,*"
said my therapist. "*How's that coming along?
Would you say it's under control?*"
"*Absolutely, Doc,*" I said. "*I hardly
even think about lemons anymore.*"
"*Good,*" he said. "*That's good.*"

Dark Glasses

**Lemon Town**
Having suffered from depression,
I'm very attuned to people's moods.
And when I notice someone's in a bad mood,
I don't dawdle; I take immediate action.
I say,
"*Uh-oh. Looks like someone's down
in Lemon Town—and they could use a squeeze!*"
Whenever I go somewhere, I always tell people
where I'm going.
Just in case I don't make it back.


**Channel Cats**
I'm a fan of
river-bottom blues,
but I can't stay
down there too long
It can get dangerous.

Dan Hendrickson

## Dominick Smetana R.D.

I was feeling under the weather,
so I decided I'd better go see
my doctor.
He has a little office out
by the truck stop.
"*Doc,*" I said, to get the
ball rolling,
"*it . . . it hurts when I pee.*"
I waited a beat before adding,
"*But it hurts a lot more
when I don't!*"
He shook his head and muttered,
"*How many times can I say it?
I'm not a doctor. I'm not.*"
But he said it real quietly, almost like
he was talking to himself or someone
who just wouldn't hear.
"*Ok, fine,*" I said. "*Twist my arm.
I'll take my clothes off.*"
"*I never asked you to—*" he began to say.
Moments later, I tossed my underwear aside
and did a little sashay.
"*There,*" I said. "*Are you happy?*"
"*No,*" he said. "*I'm really, really sad.*"
I turned around and bent down to fish
my cigarettes from my jacket pocket.
It took me a long time to find them.
When I turned back around
his head was buried in his hands.
Shrugging, I lit my cigarette.
I couldn't argue with him.
Life is sad.
That's something they don't teach you
in Medical School.
No, that's something you have to learn
for yourself
out on the street.

Dark Glasses

### Efficacy
I like to learn new words,
and I'm a big believer in using
new words accurately,
in sentences, to help make the
definitions stick.
Take a word like 'ineffable,'
for instance.
*"In high school and college,
I was basically ineffable."*

Ineffable.


### Abbey Road
No one ever believed me,
but I really did have an English
girlfriend all the way
through college.
True, I didn't see her often,
but my memories of her
are still quite vivid.
There's no way anyone could
ever forget a girl like
Abbey Westminster.

Dan Hendrickson

**Purée**
Whenever someone I know,
who happens to be in a relationship,
tells me they're going
on vacation with their spouse
or partner
I immediately picture them
"doing it" (like the kids like to say)
in every conceivable fashion.
Then when they return and
begin to tell me
all about their trip, I shout,
*"Stop it! Just stop—before you even start!*
*I don't want to hear about your*
*twisted sex romp.*
*Some of us are still*
*pure at heart!"*


**Cabaret Voltaire**
Vacation sex,
with somebody you care about,
is maybe the best thing ever.
You don't know
anyone and they don't
know you.
What do you care?
What do they care?
It's the best of all possible
worlds!

# Dark Glasses

**The Wastelands**
If you knew what people
did in the privacy of their own homes,
you'd never
visit anyone.
Not ever again.
You'd just stand out on
the street in front
of your friends' houses
and shiver.
Or else you'd turn around
and keep walking
until nothing
looked familiar.


**Every Town's a Blur**
For me, taking off my glasses
and then going for a walk
is like being on vacation.
Nothing looks familiar to me
at all and the people, they're a mystery.
Who are they? Where are they going?
What the hell do they want?
—What the hell do they need?
Of course, these are the questions
I'm always left with,
even when I can see.

Dan Hendrickson

**Pancho and Lefty**
There's that old saying:
The left hand doesn't know
what the right hand is doing.
But I don't know
how accurate it really is.
My left hand
always knows
what my right hand
is doing.
It's like, "*Okay. Alright.
Come on now.
That's . . . that's quite enough
of that.*"
My left hand's like C-3PO
My right hand is Chewbacca.


**Nonsense and Sensibility**
If something doesn't make sense,
I'm against it.
And if something makes sense,
I'm for it.
Unless it makes
too much sense.
Then I'm against it.


**Let's Be Clear**
Squeezing fake lemons
doesn't get you
lemonade.
I think you know what I'm saying.

### Shopping List

I'm not the kind of guy
who hangs around
the produce aisle squeezing lemons
for uncomfortably long periods of time.
Alright, that's not completely accurate.
Here's where things stand currently:
I can still visit the produce section
at my local grocery store, but the
produce manager says if I so much
as glance at a lemon,
he's calling the police.
I tend to believe him.

### Year of the Cat

If you're trying to meditate
and a cat
brushes up against your leg,
pet the damn cat.
Your mind's not
going anywhere, now,
is it?

Dan Hendrickson

**Panic Cooking**
The sweet smell of syrup always
brings to mind the time
I had that panic attack
at Pannekoeken.
At the onset, it seemed
so very simple.
All I wanted
was some warm pancakes,
with fresh butter
and a bit of down-home
hospitality.
But no.
No.
NO!


**London Calling**
*"I'm sick of these pants.*
*I'm sick of everything!"*
Boy, if I had a cold nickel
for every time I've said those words,
I'd be wearing short pants and
sipping lemonade down at
Lime Street Station.
Just taking in the breeze.

## Trough

If I could, I'd like to go back in time
to the moment I decided to
become a poet.
If I could, I would say,
to my younger self,
"*Why stop there? Why not
go the whole way
and become a unicorn?*"
Then I'd smile kindly.
After all, you can lead a horse to water.
How could anyone know
he'd turn out to be
a submarine?


## Restaurant Management

When you're having a panic attack
in a restaurant,
the best you can do
is manage the experience.
When it comes time to place
your order, you adjust.
Instead of ordering food,
you say, "*If I can just have
a little ice water and some fresh air,
I think that will do it for me.
Oh, and can you maybe do something
to make it so it doesn't feel
as though my heart's about to pound
its way out of my chest?*"
Then stare down at the menu before adding,
"*And if I could get a
slice of lemon with that water
. . . that would be the best.*"

Dan Hendrickson

**Fact of the Matter**
It's tough to discipline trout.
You can't send them
to their rooms.
They're already in their rooms!

**The Logical Song**
I don't believe
in tangible dreams,
the kind
you can write down
on paper.

**Swimming to Cambodia**
Every morning I wake up
I look at myself in the mirror
and say, "*Don't be a negative trout.
Stick to the middle of the stream.*"

*If your heart is knocking . . . let it out.*

**Crazy Town**
My therapist and I
were close to finishing up
one of our sessions
when his cellphone rang.
He held a finger up in my direction
and answered.
"*Hello? No, I know,*" he said. "*Don't worry.
Give me ten minutes.*"
He gave me a thumbs-up, then added,
"*Yep, the train is just about to leave
Crazy Town.*"
There was a pause and then he said,
"*You got it: Clucka-clucka. Cuckoo! Cuckoo!*"
A big smile on his face, he ended the call.
Then he said, "*Okay. Now tell me more about
this goldfish you lost when you were a boy.*"
"*I never had a goldfish,*" I replied firmly.
"*Not once.*"
He started paging through his notepad.
"*Are you sure? Because I could swear you
were just talking about your goldfish . . .*"
I looked at the clock and muttered,
"*Clucka-clucka. Cuckoo! Cuckoo!*"

# Community Cards

## We the People

I was in a full lather,
defending my God-given
Constitutional Rights.
"*Listen here,*" I said, "*it's a fact:
I sleep naked.
And I won't apologize for that.
Not to you, not to the District Attorney,
not to anyone!*"
And I wished right then that
Daniel Webster himself was there
to hear my stirring and eloquent defense.
"*That's terrific, Sir,*" said the State Trooper.
"*But I really just need to see your Driver's License
and proof of insurance.*"

## Liberty Balls

History books don't talk about it,
but the fact of it is, Benjamin Franklin
liked to strut around Independence Hall
naked as a jaybird
while the Constitution
was being drafted.
He was constantly looking for high-fives,
too, but the other Founding Fathers
always left him hanging.
Literally.
They knew where that hand
had been and where
it would
soon be again.
Ben Franklin never once
let it get him down, though.
He knew that freedom wasn't free,
(neither are tangerines)
and that nobody would ever truly
be free until we were all
free from monarchs,
pants and tyranny.

# Dark Glasses

## Men's Warehouse

Some time ago, I heard
that the spokesperson
for Men's Wearhouse
was let go—fired.
And he was the founder
of that company and its longtime
CEO.
To me, that's America,
right there.
Anyone can lose their job,
anytime, anywhere.
No rhyme,
no reason.
That's freedom.

## M'Kay Ultra

My first flu shot
was the best.
The nurse was about to
give me my shot when
another nurse came in
and handed her a new syringe.
Then my nurse used that needle
to give me the shot before
they both left the room,
closing the door behind them,
and then began to observe me
through a small rectangular
window.
I remember thinking
how great it was
to live in a country
where things like this
could happen—to anyone.
Home of the brave.
Land of the free!

Dan Hendrickson

**Sea to Shining Sea**
Here in America,
we don't have a tyrant.
We have millions of 'em!


**Gross National Product**
We took our eye off the ball
a long time ago.
We stopped focusing on
real progress and the idea of better lives
for everyone.
We got away from justice, innovation
and concrete achievements
and instead became
obsessed with the economy
and jobs,
busyness for the sake of busyness,
punching clocks endlessly, all
in the name of industry.
And so we produce little
but misery.


**Status Update**
I'm a big fan
of doing things
the same way
over and over and over again.
Everything's going so
well.
Why change a single thing?

### Small Disclaimer
In America,
you're free to
say what you want
—just watch what you say.


### Instructional Mechanism
I've heard that some classrooms
are utilizing robots now to teach children.
Though I'm not a techie (per se),
I'm actually all for this concept.
In addition to being a useful form of
alternative learning,
it will give our kids
a general idea
of how
soulless they'll have to be
to survive
in today's
modern world.


### Freedom is a Ticking Clock
If I were to ask people
what this country is about,
I'm sure many would say
freedom.
My question, then, would be,
*"Freedom for who?"*
And I'm fairly sure the answer
would be, *"Freedom for everyone."*
Which would lead me to ask
a final question:
*"Then when?"*

Dan Hendrickson

**Burrito Manor**
Around the time
The Berlin Wall
said Goodnight Moon,
I was in a writing
class with a young woman
who chose to write
a poem about this landmark
occasion.
As poems go, it was fine
enough, I suppose.
As good as any other.
It had something to do with her
reaching out to a young man
on the other side of the wall
and urging him to
allow her
to 'lead him
to freedom.'
There was a part of me that thought,
"*Well, now that's real nice.*"
And another part of me
that thought,
"*Run, comrade, run!*
*Before we tear you down*
*and build a Taco Bell*
*where you used to stand!*"
You could say I
was conflicted—and still am.


**Myth of Sisyphus**
Drowning in freedom,
still don't know how
it tastes.
The alarm rings
every day.

**Subterfuge Mill**
There's gold in the mine
and a chance
to get squished.
You take the one
with the other.
I guess.


**Fixing a Hole**
America can be a tough go.
You can pour your
heart and soul
into something
and nobody cares
or gives so much as a whit.
But eventually there comes a time
when you stop caring too.
And maybe that's
where true freedom begins.
I'll let you know.
when I figure it out.

I'm still working on it.

Dan Hendrickson

**Fair Play for Cuba**
People will forget what you did,
but they will remember what you said,
and they will use your own words
to hang you, every single
chance they get.
That's just how it is.
It's human nature.
It's an unwritten law.
It's why the pilgrims
abandoned ship
and waded ashore.


**American Express**
Silence defines you
but words pay the bills
and then always lead
to more charges.

## Cold Beat

A friend of mine once posted
on Facebook
that *'Dancing makes people happy.'*
I liked that.
It made sense to me, right then.
But, in a different mood
I might have amended that
sentence to read, *'Dancing makes
some people happy.'*
Or, *'Some dancing makes people happy.'*
*'Some dancing makes some people happy'*
might have also occurred to me,
again, were I in a different mood.
Or even, more plainly,
*'Life off the dance floor is sad.'*
But I would catch myself
right then,
regardless of my mood
and finish by changing that
sentence to *'Life is joyous.'*
We must always
remain open
to that
possibility.
Even on a world
such as this.

**Musty in Demphis**
They can't yet legislate
the blues, which
is a good thing.
These fuckers
would ruin them.


**Blue Sucker**
Wishing your blue sucker
was red
doesn't do you
much good.
Your sucker is blue, muchacho.
So you might as well
suck it.


**Room for Improvisation**
Tyranny
is 1-2-3.
Freedom
is the blues.

# Dark Glasses

**Gig Economy**
We all have our roles
to play
in Lifes Rich Pageant.
Now, these may
or may not be
the roles we were born
to play, but hey,
it's a gig.
You take your paycheck
and you try to burnish your résumé.
And you remember things could
almost certainly be worse.
You could be stuck licking floors
down at the Cat Puke Saloon.
That's what I always tell myself.


**Drift Net**
Having a job these days
is a lot like being
a whaler probably was,
back in the day.
Deep down, you hope
you don't so much
as even see a stupid whale.
But you also know you
won't get paid
unless and until you lance,
pierce and drag
one of the oily buggers
back to the bay.
Whales, you could say,
are lucky.
They at least have a chance
to swim away.

Dan Hendrickson

**Kenny Understand**
A man's
gotta do
what a man's
gotta do.
Unless he stops for
a single minute to think about
what he's doing,
and why.
Then there's at least
the slightest chance
he might actually
do the right thing.


**Breaking the Code**
To be fair, we (men) are so loaded up
with conflicting commands
and pre-loaded subroutines—
*Be strong!*
*Show your emotions!*
*Take it like a man!*
*It's okay to cry*
—it's a wonder we can get out of bed
in the morning
and pour a bowl of Wheaties
without melting down completely.
Which doesn't excuse a goddam thing,
of course.
Sometimes being a man is nothing more
than learning to overwrite
your basic programming.

### Fico Matter
I love how people's lives are
so easily calculated—into a neat
credit score by people
or machines we will never so much
as once see.
That sounds like freedom
to me!

### American Airlines
Most people don't live
in America.
Rather, most people
live in various states
of desperation.
In this, at least,
we are United.

### Progress is Never Easily Measured
I told my therapist that I didn't even
think he was listening to me.
He turned his attention from the TV and
his 'programs,' which he was catching up on,
and asked how that made me feel.
*"Not good,"* I said. *"Kind of sad, really."*
He smiled then and said we were
making progress,
before turning his attention back
to the television.
That didn't make me feel better, either.
I sniffled and asked for a Kleenex.
He handed me a moist Towelette.

*"Clowns are the pegs on which the circus is hung."*
—P.T. Barnum

Dan Hendrickson

**Theorem**
Freedom is a frown
at a parade.
Freedom
is a clown
in a museum.


**Yorick Vacuum**
My college advisor was reviewing
my transcript.
From time to time
he would frown, then spin around
in his chair
and stare across the quad.
This was all right before the start of my
devastating, seven-year reign
as The Clown Prince of Grim.
Sitting in a chair beside his desk,
I said nothing while
the clock on the wall patiently kept time.
Finally he tossed my transcript aside
and faced me.
"I've given it some thought," he said, gravely,
"and I think that you should become a mime."
"A mime," I repeated flatly. "I should become . . .
a mime."
"Yes," he said. "A mime."
I began to protest, quite heartily.
"But I don't want—"
He reached out, then,
and used his index finger
to still my fumbling lips.
"Quiet, sad clown," he whispered,
with equal measures of pity
and regard in his voice.
"Use your body poetry to
chase the pain away."

# Dark Glasses

## THE FLOP

Dark Glasses

> *"There's plenty of dives to be someone you're not."*
> —Rosanne Cash, *Seven Year Ache*

**Dead Ventriloquist**
More than once, people
have approached me
after one of my poetry readings
to ask for their money back.
But a handful of folks have
bent my ear to say things like,
*"I don't want to say your writing
inspires me, because it doesn't.
But it doesn't un-inspire me
—if that makes any sense?"*
And it's comments like these
that have made it all worthwhile.
All of the pain
and at least some
of the suffering.

Dan Hendrickson

**Butcher Shop**
Carving up a dead clown
is always dicey.
No pun intended.
You honestly don't know whether
to laugh or cry.
Either way, it's something to see.
A wound scraped clean.
Scars covered over
by a thin layer of powder and paint.
I imagine it's like everything else.
Everyone has to make up
their own minds about what it was
and what it meant.
The difference between comedy
and tragedy can and often does
hinge
on an all but imperceptible
grin.

*All it takes is paint to liberate a clown.*

**Jurisprudence**
After self-publishing
yet another book of my own poems
awhile back,
I decided it was high time I reached out
and did some networking with other 'real' authors
not unlike myself.
Authors like John Grisham,
just for instance.
I'd call him up out of the blue
and say things like,
"*Johnnyboy, it's Dan—Dan Hendrickson.
Now, before
you go flying off the handle—again—
I want to say one thing:
You write a mean legal thriller.
Let me just say that.*"
And he would generally reply by saying stuff like,
"*Listen, you idiot!
Just because you self-published
a stupid book or two, that doesn't mean
you can call me anytime you feel like it.
Do you hear me? Am I getting through to you?
And how did you get this phone number?
How does this keep happening?!*"
Johnny Grisham.
What a madman.

Dan Hendrickson

### Bitter Prison
Having been an irritable person
at various times in my life,
I'm incredibly sensitive to people
showing signs of frustration.
When I pick up on this behavior, I walk up
to the person, place my hand
on their shoulder and say,
*"Come, friend, please; don't let your heart
be a lemon prison."*
It's probably lucky I'm still alive,
when I stop to think about it.


### Rainy Day Women
Awhile back, I bought an umbrella.
That same day, I got mugged
and the bad guys took my wallet
and my new umbrella.
I decided to walk to the police station
to file a report.
On the way there,
it started to rain.


### Plainsman Motel
One night, my friend, who's
a plainclothes detective,
stopped by after work
and decided to change outfits
before we went out and hit the town.
I apparently had left my bedroom closet door
open, because I heard him clap his hands
and exclaim eagerly, *"Jackpot!"*

Dark Glasses

### Night Desk
One night an actor came in
and made a report about getting
mugged. He was pretty down
about the whole thing, until we asked him
if he could reenact the crime for us.
That really seemed
to cheer him up.

### Classic
If you were to offer me
a fully restored muscle car
or one that's untouched,
run-down,
completely as is,
I would take the junker.
In a heartbeat.
But that's me, in a nutshell.
I like things
with upside potential.

### Nighthawk
Whenever I enter
a restaurant I hear people say,
"*Artist.*" "*Artist.*"
"*He's an artist.*"
Even when the restaurant
is otherwise empty.
I should probably
tell someone about that.
That's can't be good.

Dan Hendrickson

**The King of Lunch**
It's not like I need to get published
by someone else to get famous.
I'm already known at
restaurants far and wide
as '*The Guy Who Always Orders Soup.*'
Rare is the day that I begin
to place my lunch order
when the server doesn't say, "*Hey.*
*Hey, I know you:*
*you're that guy who always orders soup!*"
When that happens, which, again,
it generally
always does,
I hold my hands up in front of me,
palms open, as though to say, '*You got me.*'
Then I grin and proclaim,
in a proud yet modest way,
"*It would appear my fame has preceded me.*"
Which seems to give everyone
a real kick.
It's kind of like
dinner theatre.
We all get something out of it.

# Dark Glasses

## Ellipses
Whenever interviewers ask me
(and this happens quite often)
where I'm from,
I chuckle and reply,
*"I'm not really from anywhere.*
*The universe just coughed me up*
*—like a hairball."*
From there, I crack a grin and say,
*"See? Poetry, it just . . . flows out of me,*
*like . . . like . . ."*
Then I usually have trouble coming
up with a concrete example, so we have to end
that sentence with those three little dot thingies . . .


## Supplemental Income
After one of my poetry readings,
there are few things I enjoy more
than talking to anyone who's
stuck around to watch me hopelessly
try to hawk
copies of whatever book
I happen to have on hand
at that particular moment in time.
Or attempting, usually in vain,
to give a few of them away.
When those brave, few lingering souls,
who clearly have nothing better to do
with their time, approach me,
I like to greet them with a look that says,
'*I have been places.*'
And a smile that
all but screams,
'*And I have seen some things.*'
Then I sit back and wait patiently
for a chance
to lift somebody's wallet.

Dan Hendrickson

**Listening Station**
People sometimes ask me what my
writing process is.
More or less, there's an ongoing
conversation in my head most
of the day. Not voices,
just random thoughts
crashing about in the surf.
Occasionally I hear something
interesting
and I jot it down.
That's my process.


**All We Really Know**
I really do have an ongoing
conversation taking place in
my mind pretty much all the time.
One part of my brain will say
something like, "*What do we
really know about people?*"
And another part will reply,
"*It's easier to steal their wallets
when they're standing up, as
opposed to when they're sitting down.*"
Then I'll say, out loud, to no one
in particular,
"*Exactly. That's all we really know.*"

Dark Glasses

**Blueprint Blues**
We are
who we are
when we are,
and nothing much
changes that,
except time,
corrosion,
creative
re-engineering
or
chance.


**Scar Museum**
It took long enough,
but now I'm kind of glad somebody
went through all of the things
that I went through.
On some very basic level.
All it took to get to that point
was enough time to
put it all in proper perspective.
That, in turn, helped me find
a place for things.
It gave me a chance
to study them carefully, one by one,
and then categorize them before
placing them in boxes
high up on shelves.
The only thing I wish now
is that most of it had happened
to someone else.

Dan Hendrickson

**Townes Van Zandt**
Where I'm from,
a person didn't
clear their throat
unless they felt like
saying something.
Like most towns, it was
a congested place.
Plenty of phlegm.
Lots of scratchy throats.


**This Desert Life**
If I ever went to Coachella,
I wouldn't tell anyone I was going.
And when I got back, if people
asked me where I'd been,
I'd shrug and say, "*The movies.*"
You want the dope,
that's how I'd play it.


*I will forever be haunted by the burned-down
sounds of The Nowhere Sessions*

## Dark Glasses

**Ardent Studios**
It has occurred to me
that it's fortunate I'm not in a band.
For if I were, I would undoubtedly
be a track leaker.
What I mean by that
is if my band were to record
a particularly groovy track,
I wouldn't have the patience
to wait for our record to come out.
On the contrary, I'd be online,
leaking that track like air
from a punctured tire.
Behind me, in the studio, my mates
would be congratulating each other,
saying, '*This song's going to change the world!*'
Meanwhile, I'd be posting the song,
free to all, muttering,
"*Yes it is, my friends. Yes. It. Is!*"
A day or two later, after word
that the track had leaked reached the group,
I'd have to feign some serious outrage.
"*Who could have done such a thing?*" I would bluster.
"*Who, I ask?!*"
Then I'd pound a clenched fist
into the flat of my other hand.
I might even kick the mixing board,
if the situation called for it.
Then I'd turn to my bandmates and say,
"*Look. I'm not going to rest until I figure out
who it was that leaked this track.*"
Then someone in the band would inevitably say,
'*It was you, wasn't it?*'
And I would say, "*Yup. Yes it was.*"
And they would all depart, leaving me
alone in the recording studio.
Rock and roll
can be a cold and lonely business,
like any other

Dan Hendrickson

**Symphony or Damn**
Keep this in mind.
Life's a long
symphony.
You're going to miss
a few notes.


**The Nowhere Sessions**
I only went into the studio,
to record, a handful of times.
That's probably for the best.
They were amazingly dreary sessions.
But, as you know, I'm not afraid to go
dark places.
Especially if it's for a good cause.
And there are times when
you kind of have to be
your own matador.
Anyway, my recording sessions
ended the way all legendary sessions do:
with a grown man, wearing only
his underpants,
holding a half-empty
bottle of whiskey and
sobbing uncontrollably.
You can't put a price on that.


**Clark Kent Sings the Blues**
Recently, I was in a meeting and
I took off my glasses, to rub my eyes.
When I did, one of my co-workers said,
"*My God—you're beautiful!*"
And everyone laughed.
I hate all the people I work with.

## Paging Glyn Johns

The idea of recording an album
always interests me.
More to the point, having
a producer,
someone who actually gives
a shit
about the work that you're doing . . .
Yes, I have to say,
that sounds intriguing.
Even just in theory, it's
a fascinating concept.


## Cutting Out the Middle Man

I'll probably never make a record.
But if I did, the name of my band would be
Janeway Tin.
And even if I should ever happen
to get a book published, I doubt I'd make any more
money than I do right now.
I'd tell people,
"*Don't bother buying my book;
it will probably be a movie someday soon.*"
Then I'd tell them not to go to the movie,
because it would 'be available
on Netflix before too long.'
Then I'd say, "*Why get it
on Netflix? You'll be able to
watch it for free on cable, eventually.*"
Then when it was on cable, I'd say,
"*You watch an awful lot of TV.
You should really take the time to sit down
and read a book.*"

Dan Hendrickson

**The Girl with Kaleidoscope Eyes**
Very few people have ever
walked out of one of my poetry readings,
which is impressive, right up until
you stop to consider how many folks
generally attend my poetry readings.
It really can't be done gracefully
or without attracting attention.
Even so, I take my little victories
any place I can.
One time, though, a young woman did walk out
—and quite dramatically, might I add.
She stood up and said,
*"Spare me your trite and stale platitudes,*
*you sad little excuse for a wannabe hipster!"*
And then she left.
Which is unfortunate.
It's too bad she didn't stick
around until after the show.
I probably would have asked
for an autograph or at least
her name.
And possibly her phone number,
if I were feeling
brave.

## Dark Glasses

**Wizard of Oz**
Whenever I manage to sell
one of my books or, more likely,
slyly leave one behind
at the house of an acquaintance,
I always follow up.
I check in with them regularly
to see if they're read it yet.
Every time they tell me
they have not yet done so,
I say, "*Well, before you do,
let me know, ok?
That book is going to change your life,
and I want to be there when it happens.*"


**Cold Glance**
The hardest part about being a poet?
That's definitely after a reading
when you're sitting alone
at the book signing table
and a well-dressed couple
breezes right past you.
And as they leave, one glances
back at you, turns to the other
and says, '*God, what an asshole!*'
That hurts.
That's a real problem.
And I don't mean
just for me,
but for all poets
from Emily Dickinson to Robert Frost
to Ernest Hemingway on down.

Dan Hendrickson

**The Tears of a**
My morning routine varies.
Some days, I dutifully shave
and other days I just stand
in front of the mirror
and cry.
I hardly ever do both
at the same time, however.
I've never been very good
at multitasking.


**Life's a Long Game of Fetch**
I've long thought of myself as
a dog who brings in the paper
each morning.
And each time he does,
he gets kicked.
Well, over a long enough period of time,
if that dog keeps bringing you the paper,
you almost can't help but start to like
the stupid mutt.

*My poetry is magic; it will change your life.*
*And if you like your life, it leaves it alone!*

# Dark Glasses

**Demo Track**
I don't know much about trains.
Sometimes they pass
quietly,
and sometimes they call out
a jaunty hello.
Often they'll whistle
in the night
and it's a song of hope;
other times it's a shriek
of pure desolation.
They can carry heavy loads
across flat lands and over
hills and mountains
for thousands upon thousands
of miles.
And then there are times
when they're broken-down,
empty
or resting stalled somewhere
along the track.
Sometimes they roar,
sometimes they whine
or howl
unexpectedly,
but eventually
they all start to creak
and slow
before coming at last,
with a long drawn-out hiss,
to a graceful stop.
Hm.
Maybe I know more
about trains than I thought.

Dan Hendrickson

**Isolated Track**
Be a good boy
and bleed a good song
There's folks on your way
who'll help you along
The road won't be easy
and choices are hard
But life is a game
and you're just a card.

So sit down and shuffle
the deck.
You won't make much money
but you might make the rent.
There's plenty like you
making deep cuts and grooves.
The best you can do is bleed true.

There's some in this town
that change smiles into frowns.
But others turn red into gold.
You've got the juice
that fuels the machinery.
The bare seed that sprouts
into greenery.

*Chorus*

Writing is hard when
nothing is new
Just pick up that pen,
it's a start.
The best thing you can do
is be a blank page
and hope the right words
will bleed through.

## One Night Only
When I'm on the road,
in a town where no one knows me,
I'm a totally different person.
I'm the kind of fellow people can
really get behind and support.
But as soon as I get back home
I'm back to being the same old
miserable, pessimistic cuss I ever was.
Maybe I'd be a better person
if I were in a band.
A band that was out
on a long tour, making all the rounds.
So long as we didn't linger
too long in any one town.

## Devil's Advocate
Every time someone tells me
"*It is what it is*"
and there's a candle burning
in the room,
I say to them, ominously, "*Is it?*"
Then, while maintaining uninterrupted
eye contact,
I blow the candle out
before making
a dramatic exit.

Dan Hendrickson

**Was (not was)**
People are always talking
about It.
Whether you have It or not.
Or if you did have It,
whether you've lost It.
I don't have to worry about
that because I never had It.
I didn't really want It
all that much.
To be honest,
It kind of makes me sick.


**Fireside**
Being a poet is a lot like
being a camp counselor.
You take your readers out of
their comfort zones,
out into the wild,
and you show them things
they maybe haven't seen before.
Sometimes you keep the group
all together and sometimes you
scatter them like leaves.
Sometimes you even abandon them
in the middle of the woods and
trust them to find their
own way home.
Other times you shove them
into the water when they're least
expecting it
and then jump in yourself and
dog paddle around with them.
Then there are times when you
gather everyone around a warm fire
and you roast marshmallows.
Those are the best of times,
if you ask me.

### Clearly Defined Roles
Poets should not be saints
and saints should not
be poets.
The first reason for that
is that saints are generally
one deeper than five.
And therefore can't write poetry.
And poets need to sample—and savor—
all the many flavors
of this world,
to understand
that which keeps it alive.


### Tommy Stinson Boulevard
I like to hover
on the edge of conversations
for a long time
before dropping in
on them
like a bass line
from outer space.
"*BA-DOOM, BA-DOOM,
BA-DOOM!*"
Then I like to go back home
and watch television.

Dan Hendrickson

# Dark Glasses

### Dilated Pupil

I'm just a guy who says stuff.
Is anything I say true?
I'm not the best person to ask
as far as that.
Give your optometrist a holler.
They see the world as it is,
clearly, in all its wonder.
Yes, they see the world in
state-of-the-art
Technicolor.

### Watching the Detectives

It took some time, but I've finally realized
that poetry
is not an overly lucrative profession.
So now I'm developing
television shows on the side.
The first show I've developed
is a show called *Hey-ho, Cuyahoga!*
It's about three guys who,
slowly, very slowly,
begin to realize
there's more to life
than drinking beer.
And no matter how hard
you try to avoid it, sometimes
you simply have to wear a tie.
I've also begun
developing a second show.
It's called *Goodbye, Miss Calderone.*
I don't know much about
that one yet.
It's about a woman named Miss Calderone.
Apparently, she's leaving.

Dan Hendrickson

**Pot Calling (Walking Phoenix)**
Growing up, I watched a TV sitcom
called *Alice* a lot.
It was about a single mom working
as a waitress at a low-end diner.
She had it rough.
Her slovenly male boss was verbally
abusive.
Of the two other waitresses she worked with,
one was famously ditzy and the other was
a faded beauty queen; a brassy, saucy
Southern gal perpetually on the make.
But did Alice give up?
She did not.
She just kept on keeping on!
And her shining example taught me
more about life than Old Bill Shakespeare
ever did.
That bald, dead, pompous son of a bitch.

*"Going through life with blinders on, it's tough to see."*
—Theme from *Alice*

Dark Glasses

**She Doesn't Live Here Anymore**
No matter what I do, it seems,
the rumor that I dated a sitcom star
from the mid-to-latter part of the 20th century
simply will not die away.
And I guess there's not a lot
I can do about it.
But what I won't do
is dignify these rumors.
All I will say is that the person
in question and I did spend some time together.
We . . . shared some moments, you could say.
Really beautiful moments.
Beautiful, private moments.
If you know what I mean.


**Visualization Technique**
People might think that,
because I'm a writer,
I have this great imagination.
Which isn't at all true.
When someone tells me to imagine
something, I immediately picture
a stickman holding a stick.
Which probably says something about
me, something I would rather
you didn't know.
So pretend you didn't read that or pretend
someone else wrote it,
someone brave—and brutally handsome!
Take life by the reins.
Choose your own adventure.

Dan Hendrickson

**Trying Times**
I've tried to be aloof
I've tried to be engaging
I've tried holding my tongue
And I've tried my hand at raging

I've tried to be a clown
I've tried to be stone sober
I've tried being everywhere
And I've tried being nowhere

I've tried being cheerful
I've tried being downcast
I've tried living in the future
And I've tried living in the past

I've tried to make a difference
I've tried staying out of the way
I've tried being colorful
And I've tried being gray

I've tried to do my best
I've tried not making things worse
I've tried my hand at prose
And I've tried my hand at verse

I've tried taking sides
I've tried to be objective
I've tried to be oblique
And I've tried to answer questions

Nothing's really worked.
I'm looking for suggestions.

# Dark Glasses

**Unstamped**
I'm not really a writer,
I'm a tourist.
I have a passport
and everything.

**More About Me**
Recently,
I thought about turning
to Kickstarter
to fund a novel about
a guy who isn't really sure
about much of anything.
And the people he knows are
all like, "*Don't worry.
Everything's going to be fine.*"
And he's like, '*Not one thing
I've ever seen makes me think that.*'
As you may have guessed,
this novel
would be, at least in part,
semi-autobiographical.

**A Dark and Stormy Night**
I checked out Kickstarter's website
last night and you have to
create a profile
and a password and all that junk.
Now I'm not even sure I'm
going to write a book.
It sounds like a lot of work.

Dan Hendrickson

**Note from the Underground**
Whenever someone tells me
'It is what it is,' I reply,
"*Is it?*"
Then, while maintaining eye contact,
I take a few steps back,
onto the nearest subway car,
and continue to stare at them
after the doors close
and the train carries me
down the tunnel and out of sight.
Then I look up at the map and
try to figure out how the hell
I'm going to get back home.


**Pack Lighthearted**
You can let a clown pack your
suitcase before your big trip
to New York City.
That's your call
altogether.
And who knows?
You might have a whale
of a good time
and loads of belly laughs
unpacking when you reach
your intended destination.
But don't be surprised if
your swim trunks get left
behind or replaced with an
out of season Cardigan.
And you had better be prepared to answer
a whole bunch
of uncomfortable questions
going through customs
at JFK—or LaGuardia.

Dark Glasses

**No Sleep Till Brooklyn**
I've never been
to New York City,
and if I were a betting man,
which I happen to be,
I would lay even odds I never
will make it there (although if I *could* make it there . . .)
And that's okay.
I mean, say I did make that trip.
What would I do then
—get mugged?
Have my pocket picked?
I don't think so.
It's been done before,
a million times in the past.
Come on, guys.
You can do better than that.
Shit, even I can do better than that.
And I lack all imagination!


**The Unexpected Virtue of Ignorance**
New York, New York,
it's a juggler's town
and I'm tired
of throwing things.
No more clawing,
no more grasping.
Now
I just want to breathe.

Dan Hendrickson

**The Exponent**
Being just one person,
I don't believe that's fair.
To me or to anyone else.
How plain and dull
for everyone involved.
Why not be more?
Why not
be as much as we can be?
Who says we can't be both
a far-ranging, saltwater pirate
and a staid philosopher?
Or a best-selling author as well as
a second-rate carpenter?
As you can probably tell,
I'm a rather persuasive fellow.
Not to mention
a natural-born arbiter.


**Give and Take**
I gave my pirate friend
a new sword for Christmas
and he used it to steal
all of my presents.

## Dark Glasses

**Everyone's a Goddam Poet**
The pirate captain slid out of his bunk
and noticed a note had been slid
under his door. He picked it up.
It read: *Captain,*
*After putting your leadership*
*under close scrutiny,*
*me and the boys have decided*
*to mutiny.*
The captain rubbed his good eye
and muttered, "*Ar. I'm getting*
*too old for this shit.*"
He sighed and reached down
for his sword.


**Pleasures of the Harbor**
One of my ancestors
sailed aboard a pirate ship.
But he wasn't a pirate.
No, he cleaned the boat,
polished boots
and made sure all the pirates
knew where their shoes went.
And, if the Legends are true,
sometimes danced
for their amusement.

Dan Hendrickson

**Elastic Man**
There was a time
—boy, was there!—
when I would have
been anything you wanted
me to be.
I mean, anything.
You name it, I'd have been it
or at least tried to be.
Card sharp, knife thrower,
Mexican Jumping Bean.
But now I'm just . . . me.
Finally, truly and only
me.
And possibly that's better.
We'll see.


**Cover Story**
If this collection of poems falls
a little bit short,
that's probably to be expected.
You have to understand,
I have neighbors who stay up
until all hours of the night,
screaming things like, "*Yes—Yes!
Pierce me again with your
sweet sugar dagger!*"
Robert Frost never had to put up
with stuff like that.
Robert Plant, perhaps,
but not
Robert Frost.
And Emily Dickinson?
She only had to contend with hoot owls
and, occasionally, cicadas.
No wonder she's so frickin' famous!

### Lying Again
I'm only joking.
I don't really have neighbors who say
things like that.
I wish I did.
I'd stay up all night.
Hell, I'd make popcorn!


### The Nightfly
But if I did have neighbors
like that, I'm almost certain I would
blow it.
For when they were 'taking a little break,'
I'd probably pound on the wall
and shout, "*Come on, come on!
Enough with the tender chatter.
This night won't last forever!*"
Honestly, it never does.
It's kind of like the weather.


### The Rocking-Horse Winner
I've begun work
on my debut memoir.
I'm calling it
*Circumstance and Frankincense:
A Gemini Reflects.*
I have no idea whatsoever
what it's going to
be about.
But, I'm willing to bet
it will be chock-full
of that classic,
warped
rocking-horse logic
that has carried me so far
throughout the years.

Dan Hendrickson

**Reservoir Dog**
In the end, when it's all said
and done,
I wouldn't mind a bit
if no one gave me any further thought.
But if anyone did care to think about me,
I hope they might think,
*"It took too damn long,*
*but, in the end,*
*he held his silence well."*
That would be alright.


**Gran-Gran Always Said**
Had you told me many years
ago that I would become a poet,
I'm not certain I would have
believed you.
But one person always believed
in me, and that was my Gran-Gran.
Time and time again, she told
me other lines of work would
call to me, but poetry
was my destiny.

Okay, that's not exactly true.
Gran-Gran told me I would
most likely be a rodeo clown
with any luck at all, and if
the Good Lord was willing.

## Sweetheart of the Rodeo
My Gran-Gran
didn't really like
me calling her '*Gran-Gran.*'
In fact, she told me to cut it
out, and more than once.
The last time she did so,
she said, '*Will you stop calling me that?*
*Jesus Christ,*
*you're going*
*to be a man one of these days!*
*And hopefully it will happen before I die!*'
I remember that quite vividly.
I was 35 at the time.


## Lifeguard
If you ever happen to find
a thoughtful rock,
keep it away
from deep water.

THE RIVER

# Dark Glasses

> *"And every day is getting straighter."*
> —Gillian Welch, *Revelator*

### Running Down
The river breaks
a lot more people
than it makes,
and the river
breaks everyone
in time.

### Flotation Device
Life is a lot
like water.
The deeper you go,
the worse it can get.

**Calliope**
Most of us start out
cheerful clowns,
with big, paint bucket smiles
on our faces.
And the show carries on as
the years rise and fall,
complete with strong ladies,
bearded men and
human cannonballs.
But time's no jester.
It leaves
us with tired eyes set deep
in creases,
bodies afloat in oversized clothes,
aching hands clinging to old habits
and battered black hats emptied of rabbits.
Our backs stooped and weary
with miles still to go
and heavy loads yet to heft.
Oh, yes, it's a magical place.
No wonder the unicorns left.

Dark Glasses

**Serious Black**
My coat once contained
a fair amount of darkness.
Of course, it didn't
have a whole lot of say in the matter.
A job's a job.
You do
what you gotta do.


**Sgt. Pepper**
Sometimes you
have to
let things slide
out of focus for a time
to put them
back into proper perspective.
Any photographer
and/or philosopher
worth their salt
will tell you that much.


**Photog**
My whole philosophy is
'*Take the picture
and see what you get.*'
Magic enters in when
you least expect.

Dan Hendrickson

**Black and White**
It can take a long time
to go
from a negative
to a color print.
I like to think
I'm almost there.


**Bentley Purchase**
When I was younger, not being
included in or being hastily re-directed
out of pictures being composed
rubbed me raw.
I would fume on the edge
of the negatives.
Over time, however, my focus
slowly changed.
Not being photographed
became an okay thing.
In fact, nothing would please me more,
after I've passed, than to have at least
a few people mutter, "*That fucker . . .
what did he look like?!*"
After all, laughter is the best revenge.
Then silence.
Then a Mercedes-Benz.

# Dark Glasses

**Photo-Flo**
Whenever someone takes
my picture, I'm always
quick to add,
"*That's who I was;
it's not
who I am.*"

**Subshade Variant**
Optometrists spend
a lot of their time in the dark
helping others to see.
Writers, essentially,
do the same thing.
But for a whole lot less money.
And often for free.

**Take Two**
Actually,
I take back what I wrote.
The best revenge
of all is still
no revenge at all.
Honestly,
who gives a fuck?

Dan Hendrickson

**Bread and Butter**
Asking me not
to make an ass of myself
is like asking a motion picture director
not to make a scene.
It's our job.
It's our very livelihood,
do you understand?
It's what
we do
for a living!


**Credits**
Before I die, I want to produce
an English movie—a period
piece, complete with lavish set design
and authentic historical costumes.
I want the story to resonate and sing
and the soundtrack to soar;
violins and strings—the whole thing.
I want my highly literate audience
to experience the full-gamut of emotions;
agony, ecstasy, excitement—dread,
so much so that they remain in their seats
all through the closing credits.
Then, after the vivid yet sublime
cello solo begins to fade,
I want the credits to identify
all that has just preceded as
'*A Clyde Lemonfart Production,*'
accompanied soon thereafter
by a flat,
gastrointestinal bark.
You can chalk it up
to simple mischief, I suppose,
or the fact I'm still
young at heart.

## Dark Glasses

**Slow Burn**
I worry sometimes
about how I'll be remembered.
My legend is a long, long way from
secure.
My place in the history books . . .
highly questionable, at best.
It can be depressing to think about,
I won't lie.
But then I think about Johnny Cash;
a guy who once, very likely,
burned down a large chunk
of a National Forest.
And today he's a one hundred percent,
dyed-in-the-wool, Honest-to-God
American Hero.
I like to believe that gives me at least
the tiniest flicker
of a chance.


**May Fly**
Richard Brautigan saved my life
on more than one occasion.
For that reason, I've always felt
I should take an interest in trout
or fishing.
But have you ever pulled
a live trout from a running stream?
They're irrational, anti-social creatures.
Borderline psychotic.
No, that's one thing I have learned.
It's usually best
to keep the crazy submerged.

Dan Hendrickson

**Stream of Consciousness**
You can put an eyepatch
on a trout; however,
most of the absurdist humor
will likely be lost
on the irate, wriggling fish.
But you always were
the avant-garde one,
were you not?
Always willing to wade in
and take that risk.


**On the Surface**
I hope I never drown.
But if I do drown,
I hope I drown naked.
That way, at least
I'll get my money's worth.


**Close the Lid**
Whenever I die,
I'm going to demand
a closed casket.
I didn't like people looking
at me when I was alive,
and I sure as hell don't want anyone
gawking at me
when I'm dead.
What's wrong with you people?
Jesus Christ, get a job!
Get a hobby!
Go to Optometry School!
Do something productive
with your lives!

Dark Glasses

**Fast Eddie**
It took me a lot of years
to realize I didn't have to
sink to the bottom
of every pool I jumped into
just to see
how deep it was.
They usually have that information
painted right on the pool apron,
for all to see.
That's a very handy feature!
Yes, somebody was thinking,
and it surely
wasn't me.


**Foresight**
Me and my brother used to
go fishing off the drawbridge
downtown.
We always put extra line on
our rods before we did,
though.


**David Jones**
My inner harbor
is so cluttered with half-sunk
wrecks
I can skip across from one shore
to another without so much
as getting my shoes wet.
Believe me, I'm not bragging.
Far from it.
But it does
make for a neat
party trick.

Dan Hendrickson

**Los Angeles Plays Itself**
The Los Angeles River
runs through my chest.
Most of it has been diced up,
altered and diverted into
makeshift concrete channels.
But there's a very small section
of it that's still fairly pristine,
where the waters flow mostly
peacefully and true.
If you could see that portion,
you'd probably think, '*This is how
all of it must have been, once.*'
And you might even be right
about that.
I'm the wrong person
to ask.
That guy's long gone.
I'm all that's left.


**Fading Signal**
America and MTV
have a lot in common.
Both were started with purpose,
drive; real vision.
But somewhere along the way,
both lost track of what they were about,
or even what it was
they were supposed to be about.
It's sad, but attenuation
happens all the time
with people.
Why wouldn't it be the same
for a nation or a
music television station?

*After you've drowned a few times you get more
generous with the lifeboats.*

Dark Glasses

**The Year We Make Contact**
I've actually been working on my
autobiography for quite some time.
It's 420 pages long so far and
I'm just about to get to the part
where I hit puberty.
I've also got three potential titles
for it, all of which have considerable
merit:
*The Swordfish Chronicles*
*The Patty Duke Story*
*Songs for a Dying Planet*

Although I might actually save that last one
for the title of my debut album, which should
drop sometime in 2027.


**Just a Thought**
I think anyone who isn't a musician
and uses the word 'drop' to describe
the date a record will be released
should be charged with a felony
or at least a simple misdemeanor.

*You begin, now, to see.*

Dan Hendrickson

**Side Effect**
I've taken so many shots
over the years
I'm immune to pretty much
everything.
The constant pinpricks hurt,
but they also
offered some definite
health benefits.
Now you could offer me things,
anything really, and I could most likely
take it or leave it.
It would be akin to offering a granite carrot
to a stone pony.
You can just hold on to that
granite carrot.
I'm doing alright.
Thank you.


**Granite Carrot?**
Oh, boy.
Even I can see where
that's going.
Paging Dr. Freud.
Paging Dr. Sigmund Freud . . .


**Stable Boy**
Over the years,
I've lost
my share of races.
I know a horse's ass
when I see one.

### Ghosts and Clowns
Ghosts and clowns
are the same in that
neither are present in their
original forms.
They both also
tend to frighten people.


### Sugar Brown
I don't exactly believe
in reincarnation.
But if I had to come back to this joint,
I would happily return
so long as I was part of a soul band
called Sugar Brown and the No-Doze Players.
We'd be the kind of outfit that could play a
marathon gig
and then jump on the bus and travel 24 hours
straight through, hop onstage and play two
back-to-back, three-hour sets without missing
a single step or beat.
I would be Sugar Brown, of course.
I need my beauty sleep.


### The Sure Thing
No one's ever gone broke
betting against me.
In fact, I'm fairly sure,
at least for some,
it's been a fairly lucrative
side business.
Even at 3 to 2 odds
you can collect nice checks
if you lay a big enough bet.

Dan Hendrickson

**Buffa-Lou**
I'll dream sometimes,
and in these dreams,
there's always that
What is this? moment.
For instance, I once
came to find myself
standing behind a bar.
When I turned around,
there was a big sign that said,
BUFFA-LOU'S.
And I remember thinking,
'*If I'm Buffa-Lou, I'm going
to lose it.*'
Then some a-hole—probably one
of my best customers—came in
from off the street and said,
"*Hey, Buffa-Lou, what's shakin?*"
I was like, '*Son of a bitch!!*'
And I woke up, furious,
pulled on some clothes
and went for a walk
out in the snow.
I like to sleep naked.
As you know.

*Not every ghost has a dream, but every dream has a ghost.*

# Dark Glasses

**Grim Shenanigans**
Having a dream on a world
that's far more conducive to
the incubation of nightmares
is tough.
It's a lot like trying
to deliver fresh eggs on a route
that goes right through the middle
of a demolition derby.
Which by no means is to say
that it shouldn't be tried,
or can't at least be
entertaining.


**Plain Sight**
I never really have much
to say—and that's the truth of it.
But I'm always talking,
so very few people notice that.
It's a little like being
a chameleon.
Give me a background,
any background
— crowded or intimate —
and watch me blend right into it.
Sometimes it's not even
necessary.
I just find myself doing it
out of habit.

Dan Hendrickson

**Aquifer**
Tell me what you want me
to say, and I'll say it.
And if I happen to agree
with the words I'm saying,
I'll say them for free.
That's just the kind of guy I am.
Yes, integrity oozes from my pores
and sloughs off into the gutter.

**Highs and Lows**
Ideas are like mountain goats.
You're more likely to run across them
when you're being high-minded
and true to you.
However, ideas are also like crushed
aluminum cans.
They can be found
in the gutter, too.

# Dark Glasses

## Perchance to Dream
Not many people are hip to my poems.
That's okay.
When Colonel Sanders first came around,
no one was too interested in his chicken,
either.
But he didn't stop.
He just kept on doing
what he loved doing more
than anything else in the whole wide world
—slaughtering chickens
and deep-frying their carcasses.
And now he's more famous than
the Man on the Moon.
Proving once again
that dreams
sometimes do
come true.


## The hungry i
It will probably never happen,
but if, someday, friends and
family members sat me down
and then broke into
a spontaneous, off-the-cuff rendition of
*'For He's a Jolly Good Fellow,'*
I'd try
my best to play it off.
I'd be like,
*"Come on. Honestly?*
*Is this really necessary?"*
But deep down inside,
I'd be thinking,
*"It's about fucking time."*

Dan Hendrickson

**Collector's Item**
The road can be rocky and
you often have to put on a whole lot
of hard miles before people come
to appreciate you.
That makes its own sense.
Do you think anyone would care
about the Grand Canyon if it was
a pleasant little ravine?
Not a chance! They care about it
because time kicked the holy hell out of it
again and again for ages untold
until it became something truly awesome
and fearsome to behold.
Something that would kill you
as cheerfully as it collects
your hard-earned park admission fees.
Honestly, it rarely ever fails.
People always fall
for hard luck tales.

*Lonely is the reign of the King of Subtlety*

Dark Glasses

**Big Enchilada**
It took years and years of
careful reflection, deep meditation
and just plain effort,
but it's all paid off big for me.
For, you see,
I have finally
transcended this sad little plane
and worked my way up
to a much higher dimension.
Oh, don't worry.
I still return to this . . . place
from time to time,
when it suits my needs.
You know, for Taco Tuesday
and things of this nature.
But in pretty much every other way,
I've moved on.
Buenas nachos, mis amigos.
Adios.
Namaste.

*Life's a crunchy taco; after a while,
the best you can do is try to hold it together.*

Dan Hendrickson

**Dormant Sea**
I think often of snoozing
volcanoes, resting quietly
beneath massive mounds
of white snow.
Frozen
in a tranquil
state of grace.
To be that silent, at peace
—but with a molten
fire still burning inside,
somewhere down deep—
to not have to say
one single thing . . .
Dear God, what a treat.


**Sleight of Hand**
Capitalism is a miraculous invention.
It destroys minds, bodies and spirits,
but, somehow,
saves souls.
It's truly a magic bullet, kind of
like the magic bullet that killed Kennedy.
The first Kennedy, that is.
Not the second Kennedy that they also
killed—with bullets.

Dark Glasses

**Fairly Sure Realist (Andre Breton)**
If you look around, you might notice
our society has stopped advancing.
Oh sure, they're making all kinds
of strides
in medicine.
And we as human beings are treated to all manner
of diversions and digital distractions.
But what's the last thing you can think of that
made life easier for anyone—or better?
When's the last time you heard a politician
talk about a better life for everyone?
I'm not saying I have the answers.
I'm not a genius or an inventor.
The only thing I know for sure is that we'll
never ever get much further than we are right now
unless and until we go there together
and we start treating all people as people,
equally,
not based on what color they are,
what country they came from,
who they are,
or how much money they
may or may not
have on a computer screen display.
Now, some people will probably say
that makes me all manner of—ist's.
But that's their wholly unimaginative,
pre-programmed defense.
I would argue the only—ist it makes me
is a realist.

*Is freedom that knot in your chest?*

Dan Hendrickson

**Progress v. Stagflation**
I'm sure some, based on the
contents of this book, will be
quick to label me a commie or
a socialist.
When in fact, I prefer capitalism
to both.
I just think at some point we have
to ask ourselves if we're satisfied
with one of the least-worst economic
systems ever
or can't we at least maybe take a shot
at something better?


**New York Times Two**
Yeah, I self-publish my own
stuff.
I suppose I could send it out
on the off-chance some a-hole
sitting behind a desk
in New York City thinks
maybe it's alright.
But I'm an a-hole myself,
I've got my own desk
and I know my stuff
is maybe alright.
There is at least
that chance.

Dark Glasses

**Extra, Extra**
Sure, it would be nice
to get published someday,
but I don't sit around
thinking about it.
That kind of stuff doesn't happen
to me.
That kind of luck just isn't mine.
But it happens to other people.
I read about it
in the paper
all the time.


**Tesla**
Throughout history
we've often seen
that the messenger
has to leave
before the message
is received.


**Not Fade Away (A Henry Rifle Cameo)**
It's not a competition.
I write what I write,
you write what you write.
The world will still
end in flames.
I'm not the least bit
concerned

Dan Hendrickson

**Cipher**
People ask me what I'll do
if I offer any readings for this
collection.
Will I appear as Henry Rifle
or Dan Hendrickson?
I've given it some thought
and I'm thinking about
just . . . being myself.
No one will be expecting that.


**Moveable Feast**
There isn't much more I
can tell you.
Other than to say you can't
sit around waiting for
Friday or Saturday night
to have fun—to cut loose, you know?
If you do that, it won't be good.
Over time, you'll lose faith.
You'll lose hope.
No, to be happy in this life
you've got to learn to
take the party with you
everywhere you go.


*"It's a cocoon, from which I escaped."*
   —Apollo Robbins, to a writer (in regard to his real name).

Dark Glasses

**Vitamin A**
Like I said, optometrists
work in the dark to
help others see.
Writers do basically
the same thing.
But for a lot less
money,
a whole lot less.
Be an optometrist; that's
what I'm trying to tell you.
That's the point
of this whole friggin' book.
At least promise me
you'll give it a look.


**Grandeur Canyon**
True vision often involves
seeing things
no one else can see.
And, among other things,
that gift can be somewhat troubling,
and strange.
You don't know if you can
really trust your eyes.
It's kind of like
being alone in the desert
for a long, long time.
Indeed, rare is the cactus
that isn't at least somewhat
deranged.

Dan Hendrickson

**Ghost Ranch**
Realistically,
there isn't enough left of me
to scrape up with a spoon.
I've just gotten really good
at spreading the paint around
and gluing on fake facial hair
to create the impression
there's actually
something there.


**Independence Day**
I've thought a bunch about freedom;
what it means and what it could mean.
And I don't know if I'll ever know
what it actually does mean
or how it really feels.
But it has occurred to me
that maybe we're only truly free
the moment we become
exactly
what we
pretend to be.

# Dark Glasses

Dan Hendrickson

**This Could Be the Last Time**
The last time I saw my therapist,
he confessed that the support group
he had encouraged me to attend for months
was made up entirely of his poker buddies.
He was quick to add, though, that they really,
truly appreciated my 'offbeat comic perspective.'
I didn't know what to say to that.
Mostly I wanted it all to be done with.
He could tell I was upset, so he tried
to make it right.
"*Look,*" he said, "*I know you're mad,
but think about at it this way: if we hadn't met,
I wouldn't have a book deal. Come on,
lay one on me, brother—upstairs!*"
He held his hand out over his head and I looked
at it—and him—for a long time.
Then I uneasily made good on that
high five he was seeking.
I hate to leave anyone hanging.

Dark Glasses

**20/80**
When you get down to it,
life is a lot
like having sex with a mime.
When it's all over, if it
ever truly ends at all,
it's kind of hard to say
exactly what occurred
and what
did not.


**Foot of the Stage**
You'll have to forgive
a lot of this stuff.
All this sex business . . .
Me talking about sex
is very much like
a cactus talking about its adventures
on the high seas and legends of
buried treasure in a pirate's cove.
Still, sometimes it takes
a cactus to comprehend
the desert;
a clown to understand
the rodeo.

*Scratch a clown's face, you're gonna get paint.*

Dan Hendrickson

## The Fighter Still Remains
I don't really believe
in happy endings.
I believe in endings
where the parties involved
stagger away and then
simply hope to live
long enough to forget about
whatever it was that
just happened.
But, that's me.
I'm a romantic.


## Artistic Vision
I know I said I wished a lot of this stuff
had happened to someone else,
but the truth of it is
I wouldn't change a damn thing.
Every stroke, every dash,
every splash
of color,
that's what makes
the painting.


## Everything Must Go
My goal with this book was to write
something so controversial,
so objectionable,
people would feel compelled to burn
all of my old books.
Were I ever to come across such
a roaring scene,
I would clap my hands and exclaim,
*"Keep this fire burning, gang!*
*I'll run home and get more copies;*
*I got all kinds of 'em!"*

# Dark Glasses

**Last Splash**
My final advice to you?
Find your inner clown.
Embrace
the circus.


**Crimson Tide**
Recently, while dining in a restaurant
courtyard, I noticed the building had a tall
rectangular window about 10 feet off
the ground.
I immediately pictured myself going inside
and jumping through that window—for some reason.
In my perfect vision, I would land cleanly
on my feet in the courtyard, dust the glass shards
off my sharp Nehru jacket
and say, cavalierly,
to the amazement of my fellow diners,
*"Now, then. Let's have a look
at that dessert menu, shall we?"*
In reality, I know I'd come through that window
diced up and horrifically wounded, landing like
a weighted sack of potatoes on the patio below
before thrashing about madly in my
blood-soaked leisure suit.
Finally, after most of the agonizing writhing was done,
a brave member of the wait staff would venture forth
to hear me wheeze-out my final words
on this funhouse ride.
*"Go, 'bama, Go Tide . . ."*


*There are few things as steadfast as a wounded romantic.*

Dan Hendrickson

### Every Ghost Has a Story
However my story
ends,
it will probably be hard to say
it ended too badly.
The fact of it is,
I could have been
Boo Radley.


### Afterword
I don't know why
my hat is sticky.
I wish someone
would tell me.


### Afterwards
No one tells me
anything.
That's why I
make stuff up.

"*Don't get me wrong, if I split like light refracted.*"
—The Pretenders, *Don't Get me Wrong*

Dark Glasses

**Other books by Dan Hendrickson**
*Clean Shorts* (Very rare)
*The Portland Stories* (Less rare, but still hard to find)

**Other books by Henry Rifle**
*Shooting Gallery* (The one people seem to like)
*Bullet Train* (Good luck finding a copy of that)
*A Bullet West* (Proof of life)
*Ballistics Report* (Parts of it worked)
*Henry Rifle Slept Naked Here* (One copy, lost to history)

Confession: *When I set out to write this book, my goal was to make a Bash and Pop record.*

*Thank you for being a trout in my stream of consciousness.*

www.ingramcontent.com/pod-product-compliance
Lightning Source LLC
Chambersburg PA
CBHW021441080526
44588CB00009B/629